ECAA® Practice Test (Kindergarten & Grade 1)

Authored by Bright Minds Publishing, Seattle WA

Table of Contents

ECAA Test Description and Details

The Early Childhood Admission Assessment (ECAA®) is used by independent schools for admission assessment. The goal of this book is to provide a framework and introduction to the problems that your child may see on the ECAA one-on-one test. The ECAA® test consists of the following sections.

Section Name	Areas Tested
Section 1: Vocabulary	This section tests child's scope of knowledge, learning ability, long-term memory, and degree of language development.
Section 2: Similarities	This section tests child's auditory comprehension, memory, distinguishing non-essential and essential features, and verbal expression.
Section 3: Information	This section tests child's ability to acquire, retain and retrieve general factual knowledge. It involves crystallized intelligence, long-term memory, and the ability to retain and retrieve knowledge.
Section 4: Comprehension	This section tests child's ability to evaluate and utilize past experiences, verbal comprehension and expression, and the ability to demonstrate practical information.
Section 5: Picture Concepts	This section tests child's ability to measure non-verbal fluid reasoning ability and abstract categorical reasoning with visual stimuli.
Section 6: Bug Search	This section tests child's perceptual speed, short-term visual memory, visual-motor coordination, cognitive flexibility, visual discrimination, and concentration.
Section 7: Block Design	This section tests child's visual-motor coordination, spatial visualization, learning, motor dexterity, executive coordination of multiple skills, and the ability to separate figure and ground in visual stimuli.
Section 8: Matrix Reasoning	This section tests child's analogical reasoning, non-verbal AND/OR verbal abstract and concrete reasoning abilities and concept formation, and serial reasoning.

Tips for parents on how to prepare your child for ECAA® Test

1. Read about the expectations from your child in the ECAA ® test at
   http://www.erblearn.org/

2. Start planning early so that you can take a practice test, and get your child aware
   about the format of the test. Administer this test and watch for areas where your
   child needs improvement.

3. Take examples and explain to your child what concept is tested in each section.
   What children need most are examples and practice.

4. Administer this test in 2 or 3 sessions. Children have varying attention spans and
   they will need some time to adapt to the format of the test and pay attention to
   each section. If you child is a bit distracted, take a break and come back to the test
   when your child is fresh and able to concentrate.

5. Teach your child how to mark the right answer on the answer sheet. Make them
   practice marking the right answer.

6. Review the questions and the answers marked by your child. Explain to them
   why a question is answered incorrectly. Revisit all the questions they marked
   wrong in a few days to see if they have grasped the concept.

Section 1: Vocabulary

Instructions:

Here is a sample question in this section:

1.   What are the various uses of paper?

Read the question. Think about what has been asked in the question. Try to answer the question to the best of your (child's) abilities. Normally these questions can be answered in a few sentences with (or without) examples.

In this example: Paper is used to write or used for art and crafts or used to print pages of a book.

All the questions in this section can be solved in the same manner.

1. What are the uses of water?
2. What does a flower look like?
3. What do plants need to grow?
4. What is a birthday? How do you celebrate your birthday?
5. How do you clean your teeth?
6. What are alphabets? What are they used for?
7. What are numbers? What are they used for?
8. What is an insect or a bug?
9. Which city do you live in?
10. What is glue used for?

11. What is a jacket?
12. What is a screwdriver?
13. What is a hairbrush?
14. What is a spoon and fork used for?
15. What is medicine? What is it used for?
16. What are the various seasons you know?

Section 2: Similarities

Instructions:

Here is a sample question in this section:

1. Sparrow, nightingale and pigeon are _____

Read the statement above. Think about the similarities in the objects that are mentioned in the question and fill out the blanks in the question.

In this example, Sparrow, nightingale and pigeon are <u>examples of birds.</u>

All the questions in this section can be solved in the same manner.

1. Spoons and Forks are used for _____

2. Colored pencils and crayons are used for _____

3. Music player, television and laptop computers are used for _____

4. A car, bicycle and truck are _____

5. Rose, daffodils and dahlias are all types of _____

6. Potatoes, eggplant and zucchini are all types of _____

7. Ice creams, cakes and cookies are _____

8. Sandals, shoes and boots are _____

9. Goldfish, cats and dogs are examples of _____

10. Pens, erasers, colored pencils and crayons are _____

11. Plates, cups and bowls are _____

12. Oranges, apples, watermelons are _____

13. Guitar, violin and drum are _____

14. Mosquitos, moths, butterflies are types of _____

15. Sweaters, jackets, mufflers and parkas are used when _____

16. Soccer, baseball, basketball are all _____

17. Blue, green and pink are _____

18. Birds and airplanes have _____ that help them fly

19. Lakes, rivers and ocean have a lot of _____

20. Sheep, pigs and horses are examples of _____

Section 3: Information

Instructions:

Here is a sample question in this section:

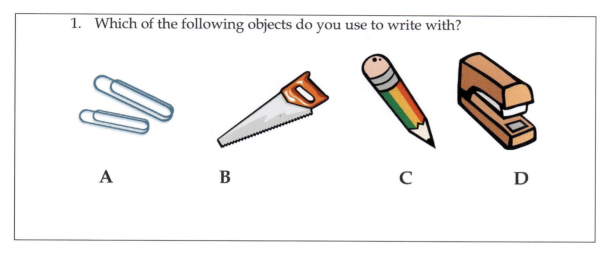

1. Which of the following objects do you use to write with?

A   B   C   D

Read the question. See the four images. Think about what has been asked in the questions. On the blank answer sheet at the end of this book, pencil in the bubble to answer the question.

The correct answer here is option C because you use a pencil to write with on a piece of paper.

All the questions in this section can be solved in the same manner.

1. Which of the following can sail on water?

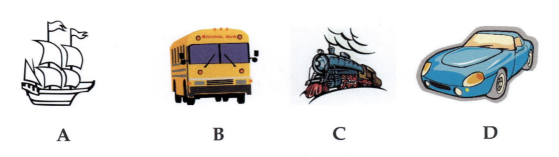

A   B   C   D

2. Which of the following part of your body do you use to see things around you?

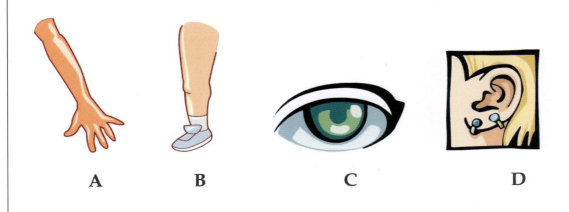

A   B   C   D

3. Which of the following images show picture of a boy who is jumping with joy?

A   B   C   D

4. Which of the following objects do you use to cut paper?

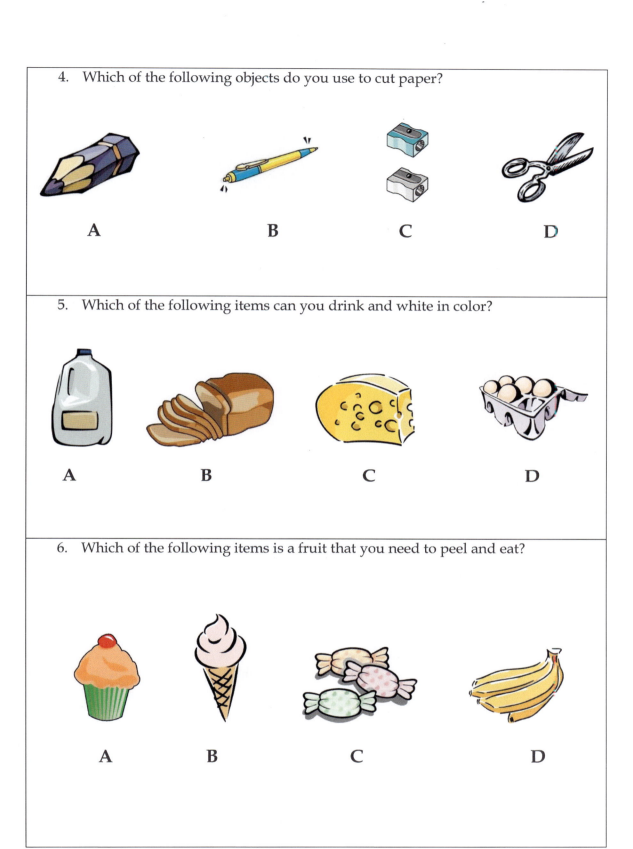

A   B   C   D

5. Which of the following items can you drink and white in color?

A   B   C   D

6. Which of the following items is a fruit that you need to peel and eat?

A   B   C   D

7. Which of the following animals can eat leaves from trees that are very tall?

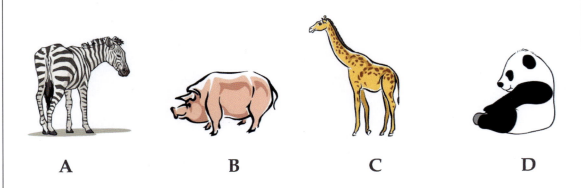

A   B   C   D

8. Which of the following animal can stay out of water and make a croaking sound?

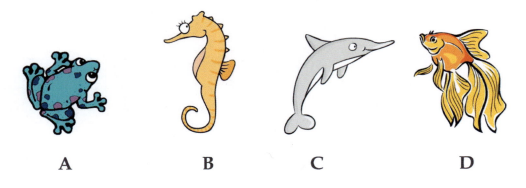

A   B   C   D

9. Identify the sport where you kick the ball using only your legs and score a point when you make a goal?

A   B   C   D

10. Which of the following would you wear to protect your head from the sun?

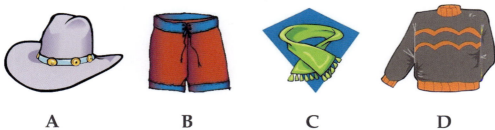

| A | B | C | D |

11. Which of the following devices would you use to work on for typing a report?

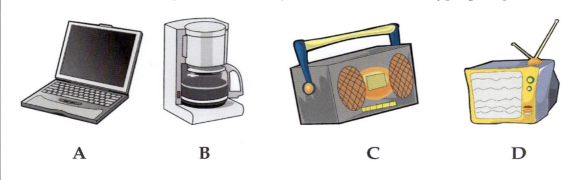

| A | B | C | D |

12. Which of the following object would you use to sleep comfortably?

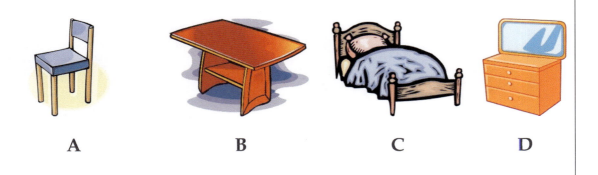

| A | B | C | D |

13. Which of the following objects has 4 sides?

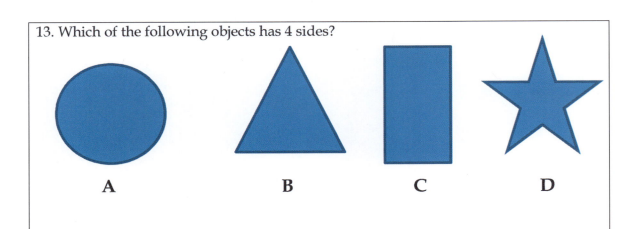

A   B   C   D

14. Which of the following would you use to put on your tooth brush and clean your teeth?

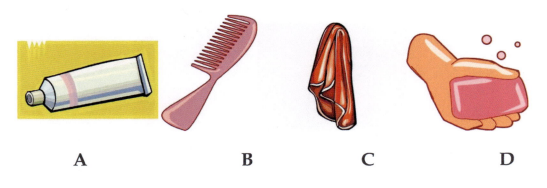

A   B   C   D

15. Which of the following would you wear to go out and walk in heavy snow?

A   B   C   D

17. Which of the following would you use to protect your eyes from the sunlight?

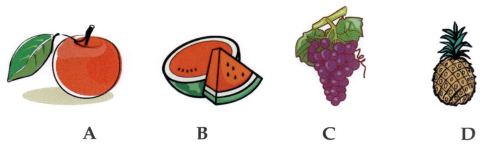

A   B   C   D

18. Which of the following has a hard and thorny skin?

A   B   C   D

19. Which of the following would you use to staple papers together?

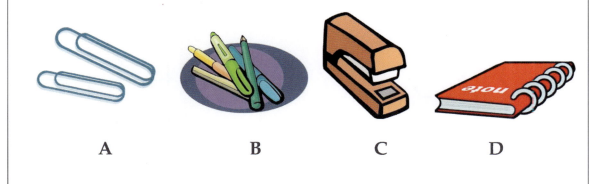

A   B   C   D

20. Which of the following is sweet and you would need to cut into slices in order to eat it?

A   B   C   D

21. Which of the following has prickly thorns and grows well in deserts?

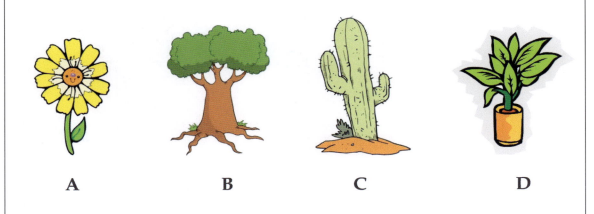

A   B   C   D

22. Which of the following lives on farms and has horns?

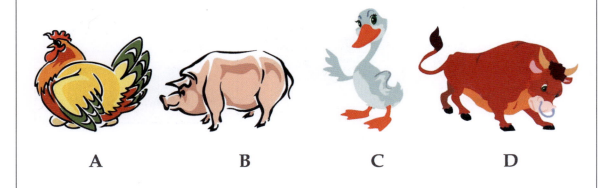

A   B   C   D

23. What is your favorite food?

24. Give an example of a household pet.

25. What toys do you like to play with?

26. Can you give me 6 colors that you know about? What is your favorite color?

27. Give me 5 examples of fruits.

28. Explain how you wash your hands?

29. What do you eat for breakfast?

30. Describe the clothes you like to wear.

Section 4: Comprehension

Instructions:

Here is a sample question in this section:

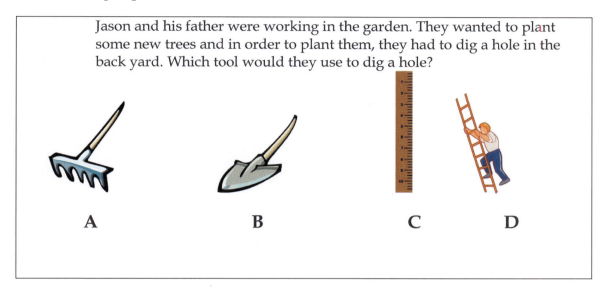

Jason and his father were working in the garden. They wanted to plant some new trees and in order to plant them, they had to dig a hole in the back yard. Which tool would they use to dig a hole?

A   B   C   D

Read the question. See the four images. Try and figure which of the following objects can be used to answer the question. On the blank answer sheet at the end of this book, pencil in the bubble to answer the question.

The correct answer here is option B because a shovel is used to dig a hole in the ground.

All the questions in this section can be solved in the same manner.

1   Corey went to the airport to take a flight to visit his grandmother with her 3 brothers and parents. When he got to the airport he saw a lot of things that took off and landed. He even boarded one to go to his grandmother. Which is it?

A   B   C   D

2.   Nancy celebrated her birthday party with her family and friends. She cut this food during her party. Each of her friends even got a slice of this sweet thing. Which was it?

A   B   C   D

3.   You play this game on a board, plan your moves and try to defeat the opponent by attacking their pieces. Which game is this?

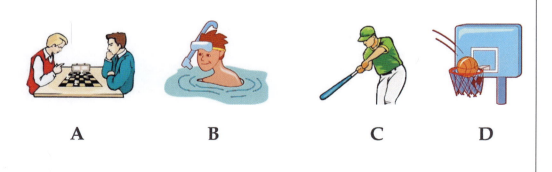

A   B   C   D

4. Misty likes to play with her toys in her room. One of her favorite toys is a soft toy that is an animal. Which is it?

A   B   C   D

5. Every evening the kids love to play on the swing, jungle gym and other play equipment in the park. Which of the following is **not** something they would find in the park that is safe for children?

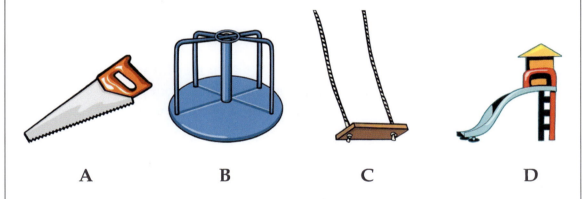

A   B   C   D

6. In order to get to school, Ann has to take a school bus that picks her up outside her house. The bus also picks up several other children in the neighborhood. Which of the following shows how she will get to school?

A   B   C   D

7. Gregory lives in Portland, Oregon where it rains quite a lot. Which of the following items should he carry with him to keep him dry while walking to school and back home?

A   B   C   D

8. After playing all afternoon in the sun, the kids were very thirsty and asked for something that they can drink to quench their thirst. What did they ask for?

A   B   C   D

9. During her annual checkup with the doctor, Amanda was told by the doctor to drink a glass of milk with her regular breakfast before she headed off to middle school. Which of the following shows the amount of milk she will drink before heading off to school?

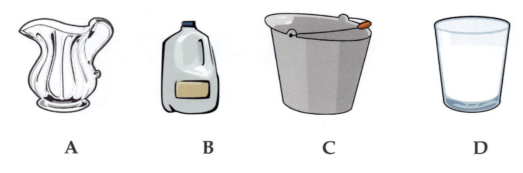

A   B   C   D

10. Tara likes to bike around the neighborhood on her new bike. In order to be safe, what must she wear to protect her head from injuries?

A   B   C   D

11. Yong likes to paint a lot with crayons, water colors and color pencils during his spare time. He draws lots of pictures and colors them. Which of the following cannot be used to color?

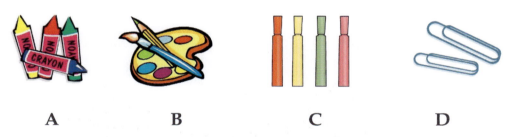

A   B   C   D

12. Cathy went with her mother to get groceries. Which of the following things is she likely **not** to buy from the grocery store?

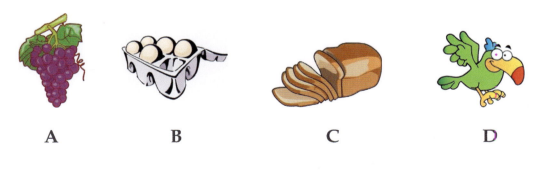

A   B   C   D

13. In order to prepare for the new year of school, Ryan's mother purchased lots of new school supplies, a backpack and other things. Which of the following will he buy in order to take his lunch to school?

A   B   C   D

14. Harry was not feeling too good. His mother and father took him to see someone who would examine him and give him medicine for his cough and cold so he could feel better. Who did they see?

A   B   C   D

15. Emily decided to plant some vegetables and fruits in her vegetable patch behind her house. Which one of the following is hot and spicy and her mother uses it to prepare spicy food?

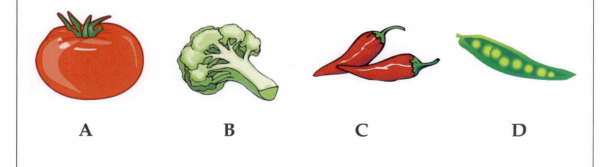

A   B   C   D

16. Jessica Johnson has a younger brother Alex Johnson. Alex is taller than Jessica. Jessica's mother Alicia is taller than Alex. Which picture below would be the right picture for the family?

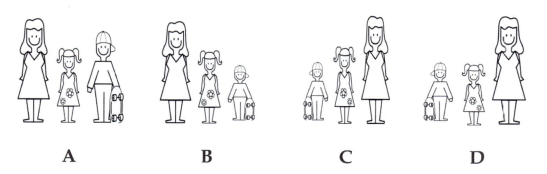

    A   **B**   **C**   **D**

17. Victoria got into trouble and was given a timeout and asked to spend the day in her room. She was not allowed to play with her video games or dolls or watch TV. Which is the one object she can use in her room during her timeout?

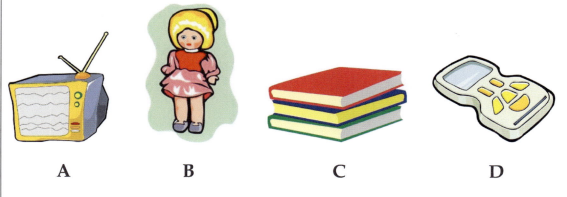

    A   **B**   **C**   **D**

18. Mary's younger brother is 5 years old. Her older brother is 9 years old. How old can Mary be?

5   9   7   11

  A   **B**   **C**   **D**

19. Rose decided to distribute 1 dum-dum to each of her three friends. She would take one and save one for her younger brother. How many dum-dums would she have to buy?

A   B   C   D

20. Newton and his mother went to the grocery store and got 6 muffins. Newton, his brother, mother and father ate one each. How many total muffins did they eat?

A   B   C   D

21. Emily wanted to help her mother bake a cake. Which of the following appliances did her mother use to bake a cake?

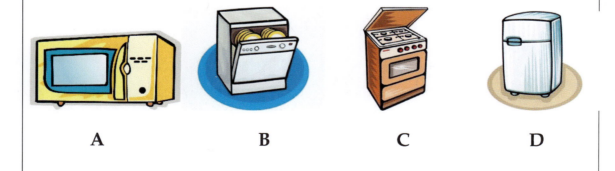

A   B   C   D

22. Rory wants to learn a musical instrument. He decided to take on this instrument that has a keyboard with white and black keys. What instrument did he take up playing?

A   B   C   D

Section 5: Non-Verbal Picture Concepts

Instructions:

Here is a sample question in this section:

#1   #2   #3

#4   #5   #6

See the images on all the rows. Try to associate one image from each row to another one based on an organizational concept.

For this specific example, #1 in 1st row and #6 in 2nd row are the performance arts (ballet and Singing) and hence form an organizational concept namely "performance arts".

All the questions in this section can be solved in the same manner.

1. Select one object from each row to form an organizational concept. (i.e one object from each row can be grouped together in specific way).

#1	#2	#3
#4	#5	#6

Objects _____ and _____ form a group because _____

2. Select one object from each row to form an organizational concept. (i.e one object from each row can be grouped together in specific way).

#1	#2	#3
#4	#5	#6

Objects _____ and _____ form a group because _____

3. Select one object from each row to form an organizational concept. (i.e one object from each row can be grouped together in specific way).

| #1 | #2 | #3 |

| #4 | #5 | #6 |

Objects _____ and _____ form a group because _____

4. Select one object from each row to form an organizational concept. (i.e one object from each row can be grouped together in specific way).

| #1 | #2 | #3 |

| #4 | #5 | #6 |

Objects _____ and _____ form a group because _____

5. Select one object from each row to form an organizational concept. (i.e one object from each row can be grouped together in specific way).

#1	#2	#3
#4	#5	#6
#7	#8	#9

Objects _____, _____ and _____ form a group because _____

6. Select one object from each row to form an organizational concept. (i.e one object from each row can be grouped together in specific way).

#1	#2	#3
#4	#5	#6

Objects _____ and _____ form a group because _____

7. Select one object from each row to form an organizational concept. (i.e one object from each row can be grouped together in specific way).

Objects _____ and _____ form a group because _____

8. Select one object from each row to form an organizational concept. (i.e one object from each row can be grouped together in specific way).

Objects _____ and _____ form a group because _____

9. Select one object from each row to form an organizational concept. (i.e one object from each row can be grouped together in specific way).

#1	#2	#3
#4	#5	#6

Objects _____ and _____ form a group because _____

10. Select one object from each row to form an organizational concept. (i.e one object from each row can be grouped together in specific way).

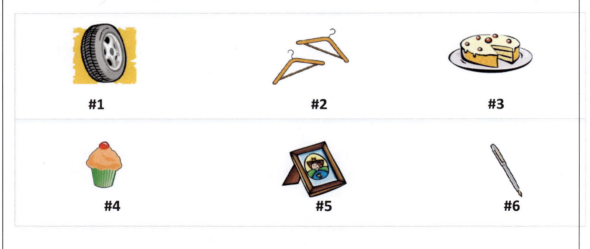

#1	#2	#3
#4	#5	#6

Objects _____ and _____ form a group because _____

11. Select one object from each row to form an organizational concept. (i.e one object from each row can be grouped together in specific way).

#1

#2

#3

#4

#5

#6

Objects _____ and _____ form a group because _____

12. Select one object from each row to form an organizational concept. (i.e one object from each row can be grouped together in specific way).

#1

#2

#3

#4

#5

#6

Objects _____ and _____ form a group because _____

13. Select one object from each row to form an organizational concept. (i.e one object from each row can be grouped together in specific way).

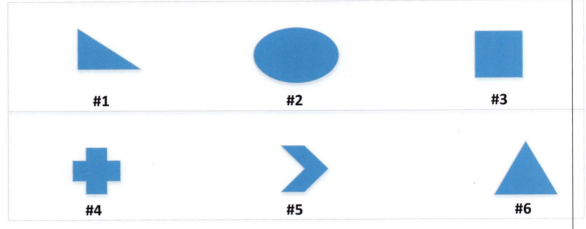

Objects _____ and _____ form a group because _____

14. Select one object from each row to form an organizational concept. (i.e one object from each row can be grouped together in specific way).

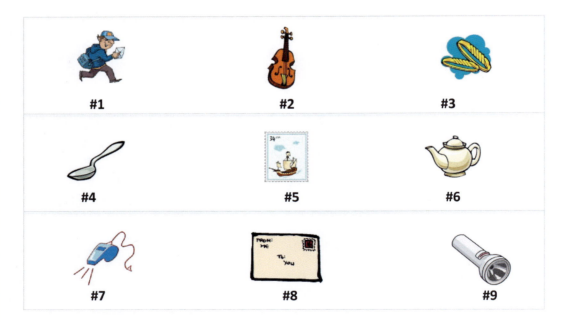

Objects _____, _____and _____ form a group because _____

15. Select one object from each row to form an organizational concept. (i.e one object from each row can be grouped together in specific way).

#1   #2   #3

#4   #5   #6

#7   #8   #9

Objects _____, _____ and _____ form a group because _____

41

Section 6: Bug Search

Instructions:

Here is a sample question in this section:

#1   #2   #3   #4   #5

Find the image of the bug labeled #1 through #5 that matches with the image of the bug inside the box.

For this specific example, the bug inside the box matches the bug #3.

All the questions in this section can be solved in the same manner.

1. See the picture of the bug inside the box. Search for the same bug in the group of bugs marked #1 to #5.

#1　　#2　　#3　　#4　　#5

2. See the picture of the bug inside the box. Search for the same bug in the group of bugs marked #1 to #5.

#1　　#2　　#3　　#4　　#5

3. See the picture of the bug inside the box. Search for the same bug in the group of bugs marked #1 to #5.

#1　　#2　　#3　　#4　　#5

4. See the picture of the bug inside the box. Search for the same bug in the group of bugs marked #1 to #5.

                                #1   #2   #3   #4   #5

5. See the picture of the bug inside the box. Search for the same bug in the group of bugs marked #1 to #5.

                                #1   #2   #3   #4   #5

6. See the picture of the bug inside the box. Search for the same bug in the group of bugs marked #1 to #5.

                                #1   #2   #3   #4   #5

7. See the picture of the bug inside the box. Search for the same bug in the group of bugs marked #1 to #5.

                       #1   **#2**   **#3**   **#4**   **#5**

8. See the picture of the bug inside the box. Search for the same bug in the group of bugs marked #1 to #5.

                       #1   **#2**   **#3**   **#4**   **#5**

9. See the picture of the bug inside the box. Search for the same bug in the group of bugs marked #1 to #5.

                       #1   **#2**   **#3**   **#4**   **#5**

10. See the picture of the bug inside the box. Search for the same bug in the group of bugs marked #1 to #5.

                                   #1   #2   #3   #4   #5

11. See the picture of the bug inside the box. Search for the same bug in the group of bugs marked #1 to #5.

                                   #1   #2   #3   #4   #5

12. See the picture of the bug inside the box. Search for the same bug in the group of bugs marked #1 to #5.

                                   #1   #2   #3   #4   #5

13. See the picture of the bug inside the box. Search for the same bug in the group of bugs marked #1 to #5.

        #1   **#2**   **#3**   **#4**   **#5**

14. See the picture of the bug inside the box. Search for the same bug in the group of bugs marked #1 to #5.

        #1   **#2**   **#3**   **#4**   **#5**

Section 7: Block Design

This page is intentionally kept blank

Block Diagram Cut-out

Instructions:

Use your parents help to cut out these shapes below. See the problems in this section and try to construct them using the shapes that you cut out.

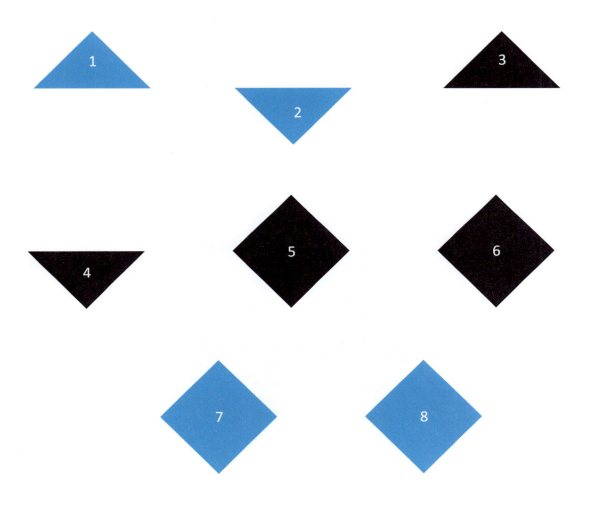

This page is intentionally kept blank

1. Using the cut-out pieces, construct the following diagram

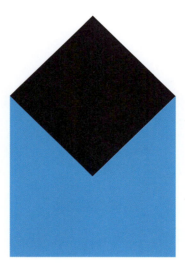

2. Using the cut-out pieces, construct the following diagram

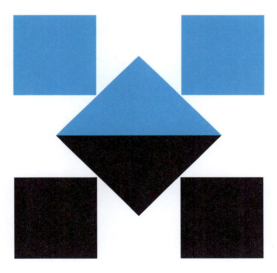

3. Using the cut-out pieces, construct the following diagram.

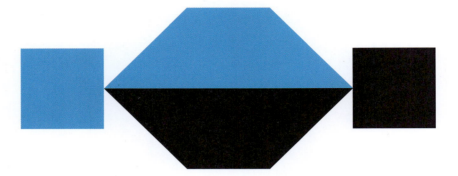

4. Using the cut-out pieces, construct the following diagram.

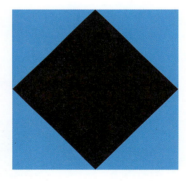

5. Using the cut-out pieces, construct the following diagram.

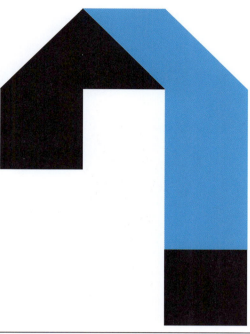

6. Using the cut-out pieces, construct the following diagram.

7. Using the cut-out pieces, construct the following diagram.

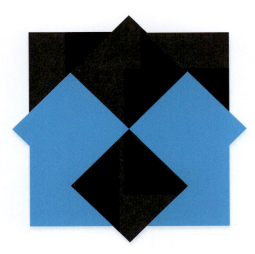

8. Using the cut-out pieces, construct the following diagram.

9. Using the cut-out pieces, construct the following diagram.

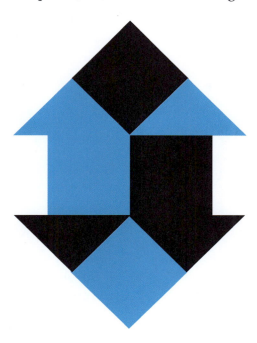

10. Using the cut-out pieces, construct the following diagram.

11. Using the cut-out pieces, construct the following diagram.

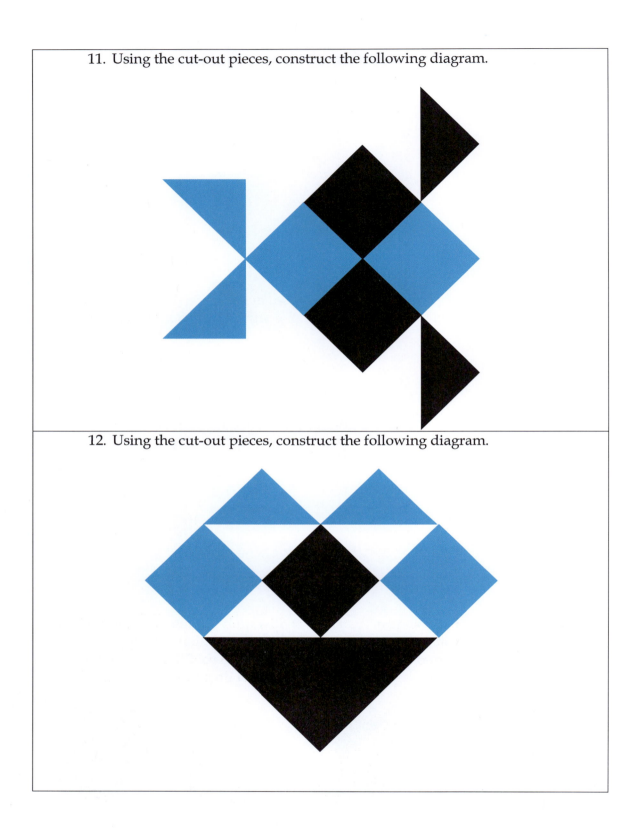

12. Using the cut-out pieces, construct the following diagram.

13. Using the cut-out pieces, construct the following diagram.

14. Using the cut-out pieces, construct the following diagram.

15. Using the cut-out pieces, construct the following diagram.

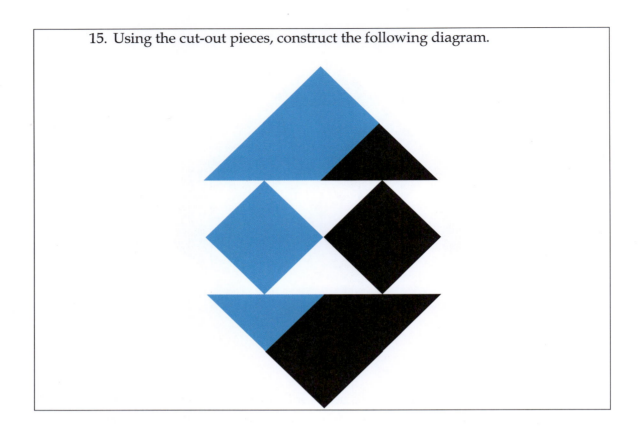

Section 8: Matrix Reasoning

Instructions:

Here is a sample question in this section:

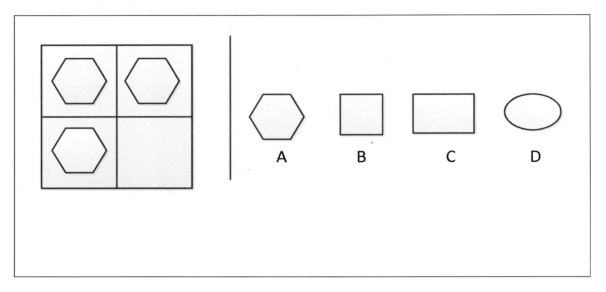

A   B   C   D

See the 3 images on the left side of the line. Then see the 4 images on the right side of the line. See if there is a pattern for the images on the left side and figure which images would complete the pattern on the left side.

The correct answer here is Option A because the objects on the left side have 6 sides and the object A has 6 sides.

All the questions in this section can be solved in the same manner.

1.

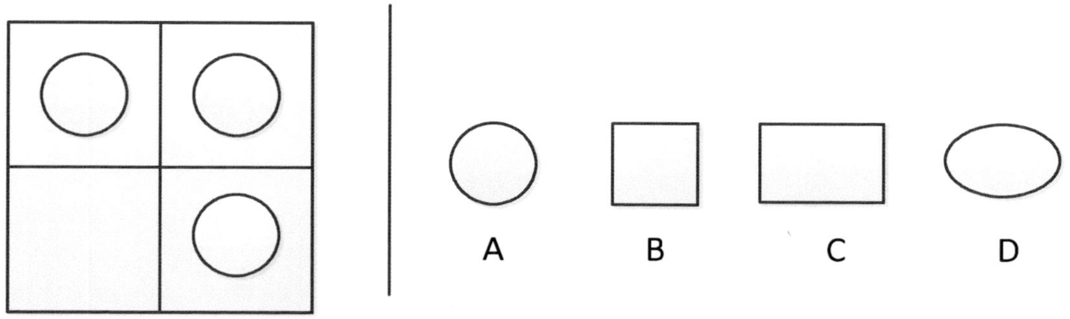

A   B   C   D

2.

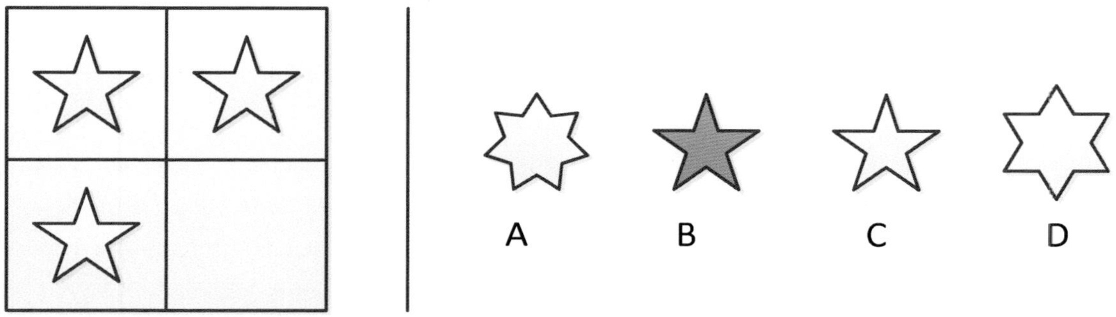

A   B   C   D

3.

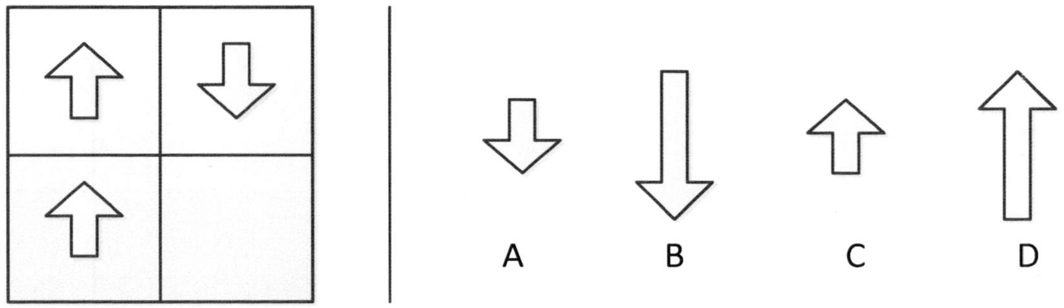

A   B   C   D

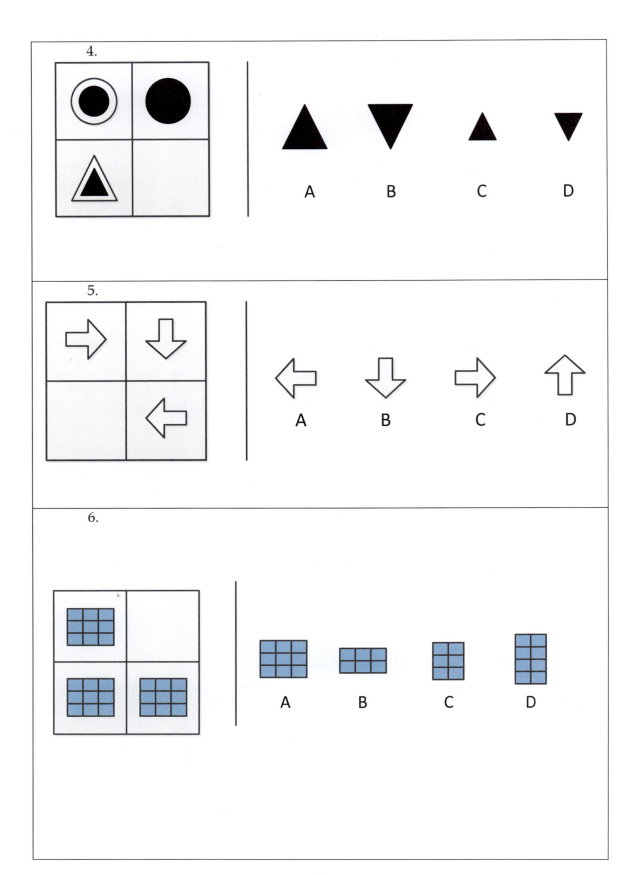

4.

5.

6.

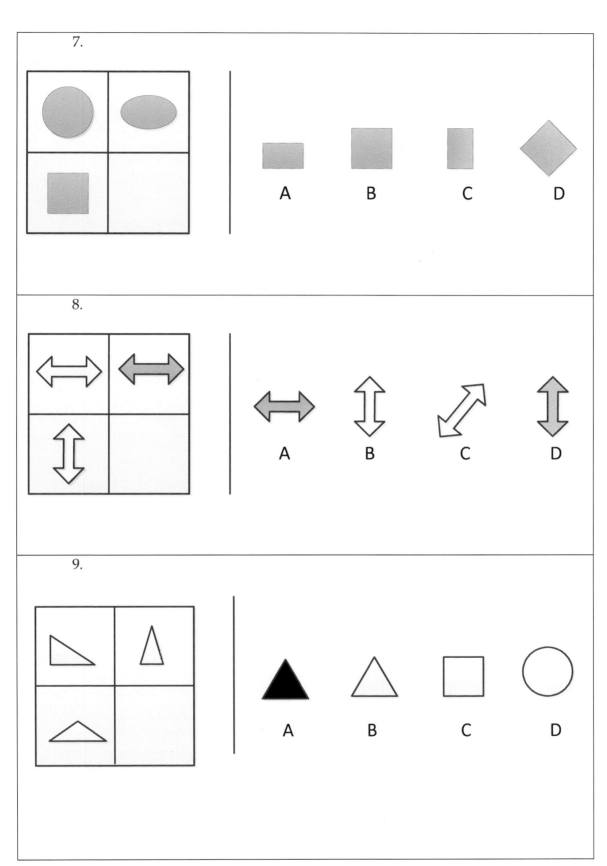

7.

A   B   C   D

8.

A   B   C   D

9.

A   B   C   D

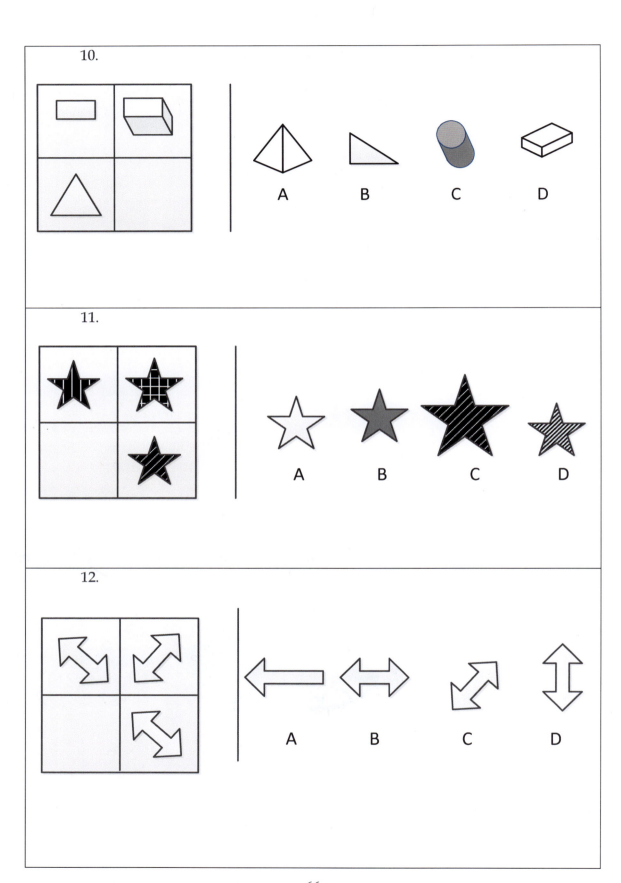

10.

11.

12.

13.

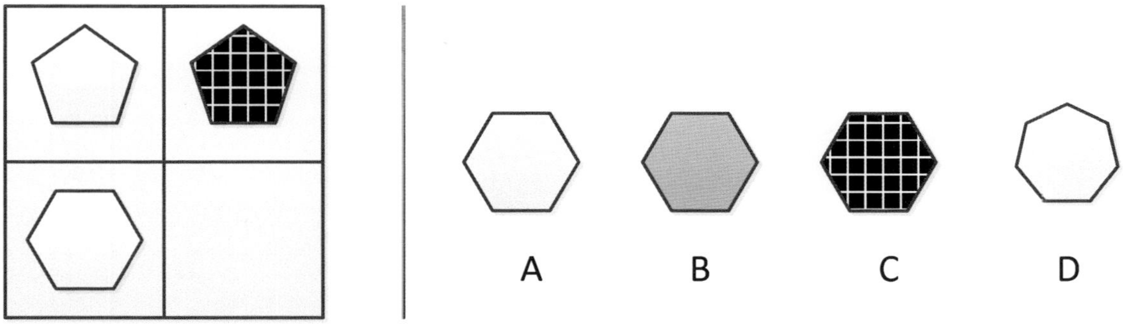

A   B   C   D

14.

A   B   C   D

15.

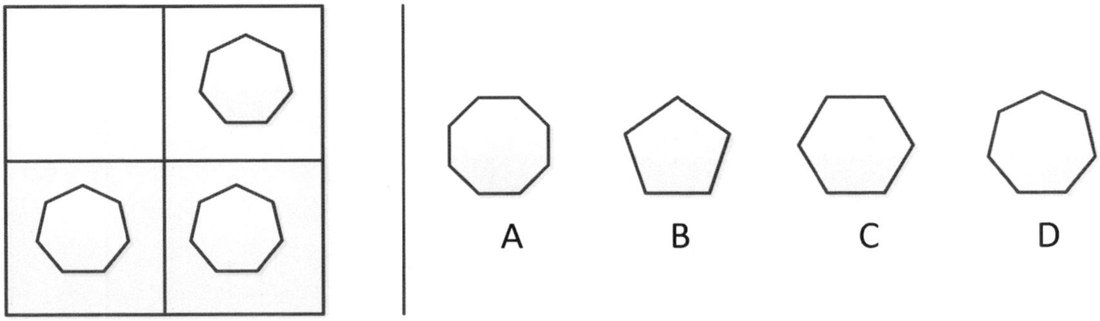

A   B   C   D

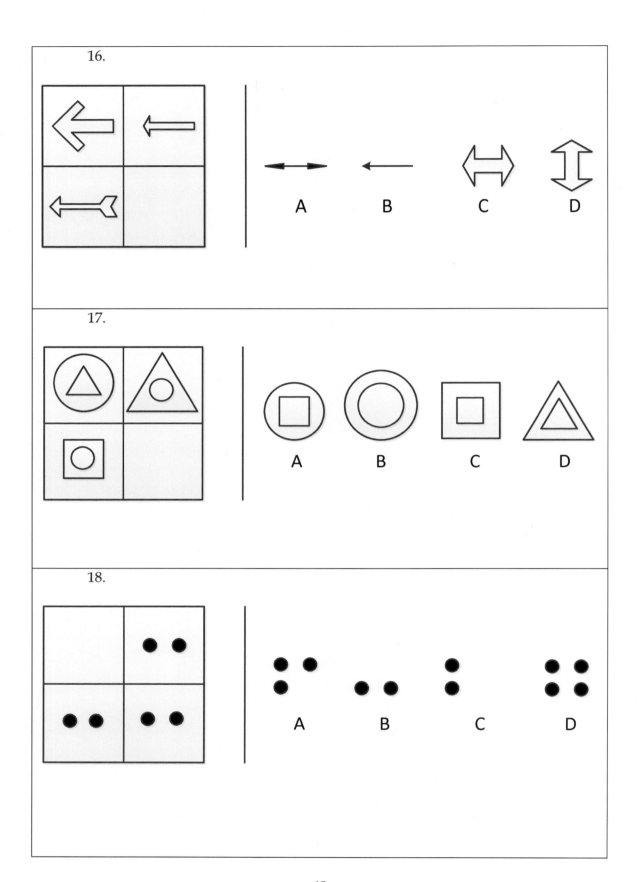

16.

A B C D

17.

A B C D

18.

A B C D

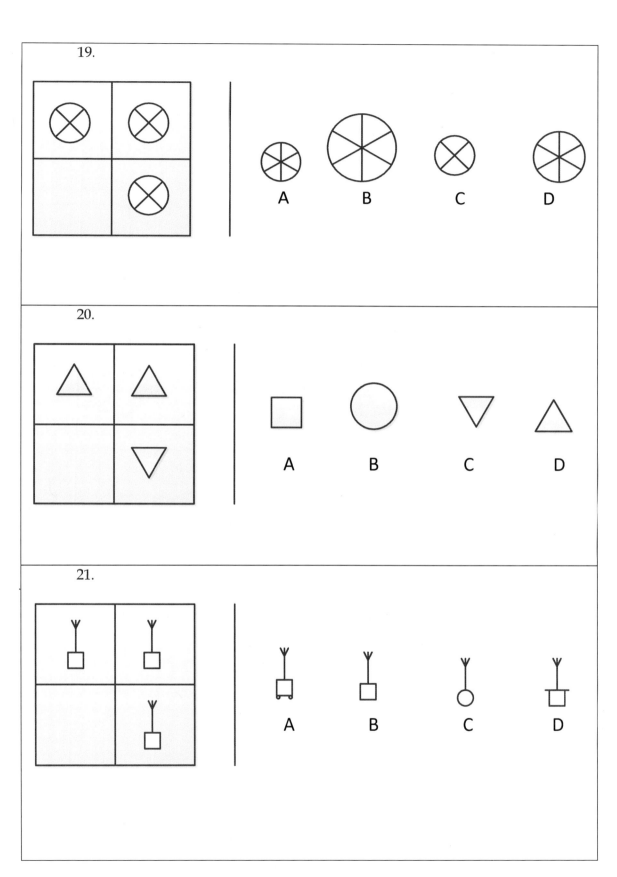

19.

A   B   C   D

20.

A   B   C   D

21.

A   B   C   D

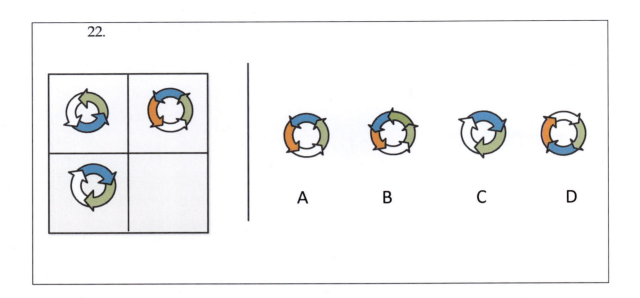

22

A   B   C   D

Answer Key

Section 1: Oral Vocabulary

There is no specific correct answer to any of the questions in this section. These are merely some hints and keywords you can look for in the answers.

1. Answer should include few things for example drinking, washing hands, taking shower, watering plants, cooking.
2. Answer should include colorful, red, blue, yellow, soft to touch, fragrant, delicate and other adjectives.
3. Answer should include walking, running, train, car, boat, biking, etc.
4. Answer should include water, sun, soil, etc.
5. Answer should include – day in the year someone is born, celebrate with balloons, party, favorite food, playing with friends, parents and relatives, etc.
6. Answer should be "apply paste on tooth brush", brush your teeth, rinse with water etc.
7. Answer should include – Alphabets are set of letters in a fixed order. Alphabets are things like A, B, C, etc. They are used to build words.
8. Answer should include - Numbers have a certain value. e.g. 1, 2, 3, etc. They are used to count some things and are used in math.
9. Answer can be any of the following – parent or parents, brothers, sisters, aunties, uncles, grandparents or other relatives or guardians.
10. Answer should include – insect or bug are small animals or creatures that can crawl or move around e.g. ants, ladybugs, spiders, cockroaches etc.
11. Answer should include the name of the city or the suburb they live in.
12. Answer should include – stick papers, craft objects, broken pieces of things – wood, cardboard etc.
13. Answer should include – something you wear on top of a shirt to protect yourself from the cold wind or rain during winter.
14. Answer should include – used to fix a screw or fasten something together.
15. Answer should include – used to comb your hair, dolls hair etc.
16. Answer should include – used to eat soup, rice or vegetables
17. Answer should include – something you take when you are sick – e.g. fever, runny nose etc.
18. Answer should include their favorite color.
19. Answer should include – how a certain object is formed. E.g. round, square, triangle etc.
20. Answer should include one of many of summer, winter, fall, autumn, monsoon etc.

Section 2: Similarities

There is no specific correct answer to the questions in this section. As long as the child can identify the proper common category or similarity between things, you have a correct answer. These are merely some hints and keywords you can look for in the answers.

1. They are used for eating food.
2. Coloring a painting or drawing.
3. Working, playing or entertaining yourself. All of them are electronic gadgets.
4. They are all vehicles and used to travel from one place to another.
5. They are types of flowers.
6. They are types of vegetables.
7. They are types of deserts or sweets. You have them at parties.
8. They are types of footwear and used to protect your feet when you walk.
9. They are types of pets.
10. They are types of stationery and used to do school work or home work.
11. They are types of utensils and used to eat or plate food.
12. They are types of fruits.
13. They are types of musical instruments.
14. They are types of insects or bugs and they have winds and can fly.
15. They are types of outerwear used to protect yourself from the cold.
16. They are types of sports. They are all played with a (different sized) ball.\
17. They are all colors.
18. They have winds that help them fly.
19. They have a lot of water.
20. They are type of barn animals.

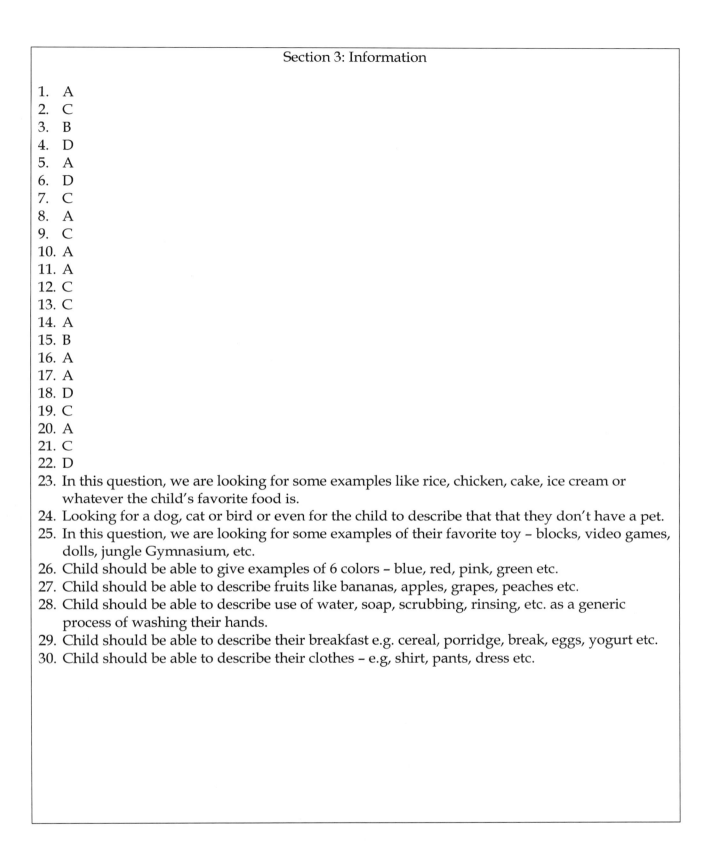

Section 3: Information

1. A
2. C
3. B
4. D
5. A
6. D
7. C
8. A
9. C
10. A
11. A
12. C
13. C
14. A
15. B
16. A
17. A
18. D
19. C
20. A
21. C
22. D
23. In this question, we are looking for some examples like rice, chicken, cake, ice cream or whatever the child's favorite food is.
24. Looking for a dog, cat or bird or even for the child to describe that that they don't have a pet.
25. In this question, we are looking for some examples of their favorite toy – blocks, video games, dolls, jungle Gymnasium, etc.
26. Child should be able to give examples of 6 colors – blue, red, pink, green etc.
27. Child should be able to describe fruits like bananas, apples, grapes, peaches etc.
28. Child should be able to describe use of water, soap, scrubbing, rinsing, etc. as a generic process of washing their hands.
29. Child should be able to describe their breakfast e.g. cereal, porridge, break, eggs, yogurt etc.
30. Child should be able to describe their clothes – e.g, shirt, pants, dress etc.

Section 4: Comprehension

1. A
2. C
3. A
4. A
5. A
6. C
7. A
8. B
9. D
10. B
11. D
12. D
13. A
14. D
15. C
16. A
17. C
18. C
19. D
20. D
21. C
22. C

Section 5: Non-verbal Picture concepts

1. Spoon and Fork form a group because they are used to eat food.
2. Brush and Paste form a group because they are used to brush your teeth.
3. Winter hat and winter gloves form a group because they are used to protect yourself from the cold weather.
4. Ship and Airplane form a group because they are modes of transportation.
5. Eyes, Lips and Ears form a group because they are parts of your face.
6. Hammer and Nails form a group because they are used together to fix things.
7. Grandpa and Grandma form a group as they are part of a family.
8. Computer and Phone form a group as they are types of electronic gadgets.
9. The Pig and the Bull form a group as they are types of barn animals.
10. Cake and Cupcake form a group as they are types of desert.
11. The Head and Hat form a group as they go together.
12. Button and Zip form a group as they both are used to fasten clothes.
13. Right Angle and Equilateral Triangle form a group are they are types of triangle.
14. Postman, Stamp and Envelope form a group as they all are a part of the postal system.
15. Kiwi, Grapes and Pineapple form a group as they are types of fruits.

1. Matching bug is #5
2. Matching bug is #3
3. Matching bug is #4
4. Matching bug is #2
5. Matching bug is #2
6. Matching bug is #4
7. Matching bug is #4
8. Matching bug is #4
9. Matching bug is #1
10. Matching bug is #3
11. Matching bug is #5
12. Matching bug is #3
13. Matching bug is #4
14. Matching bug is #3
15. Matching bug is #3

1.

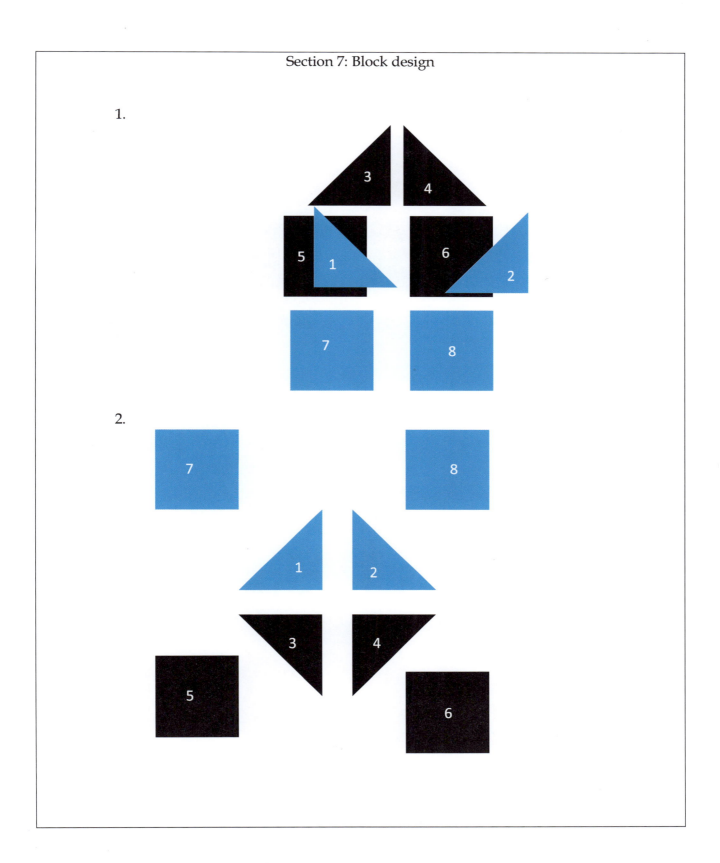

2.

3.

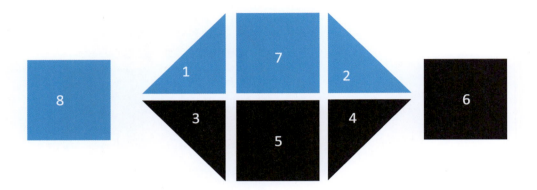

4.

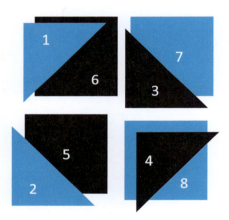

5.

6.

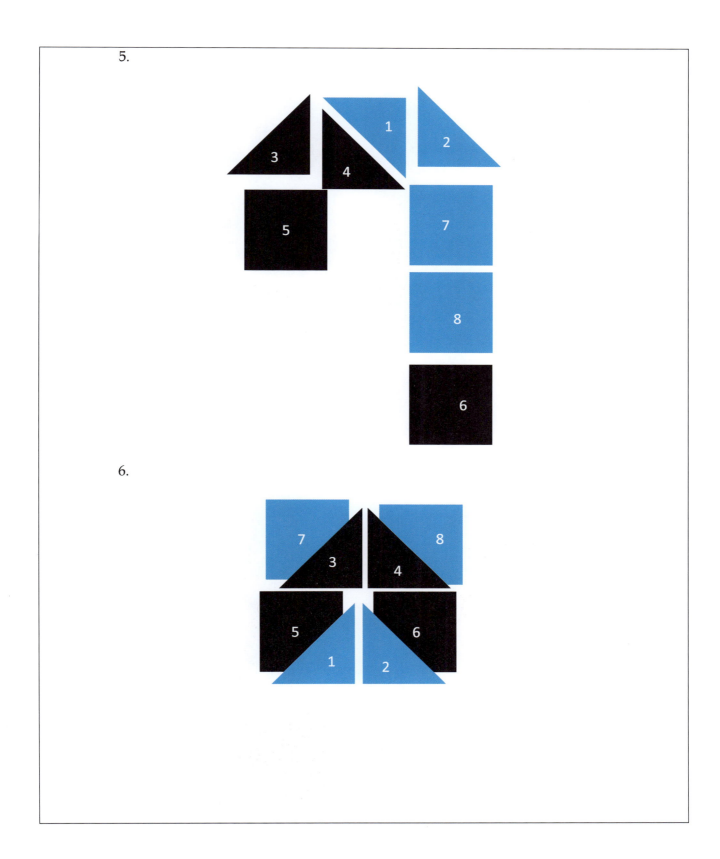

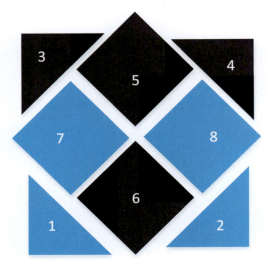

7

8.

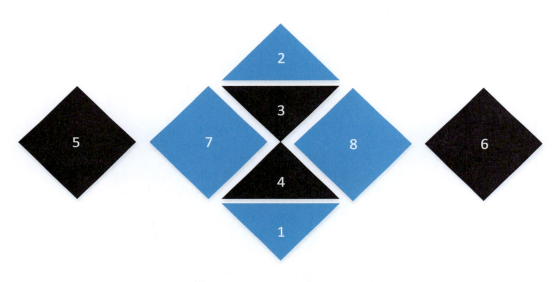

9.

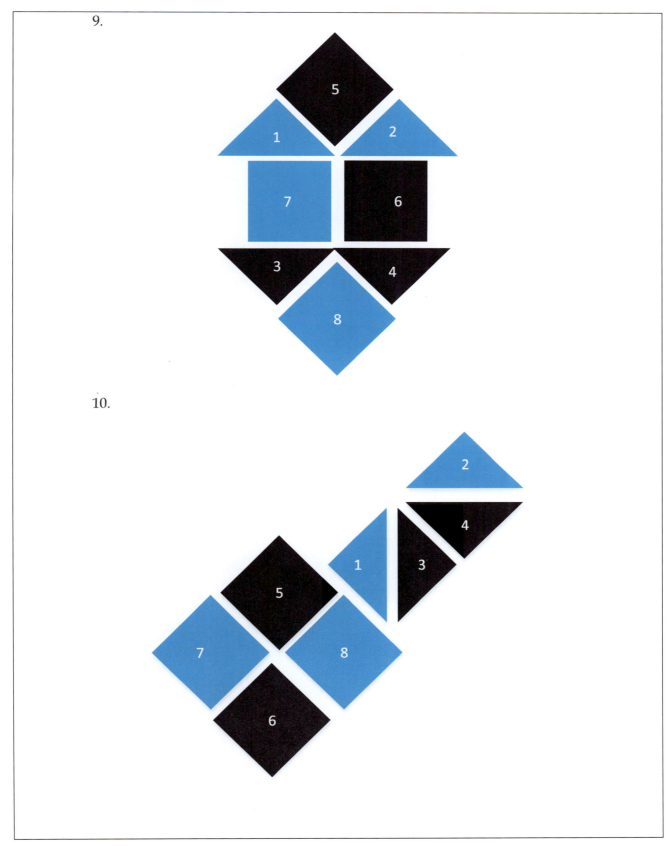

10.

11.

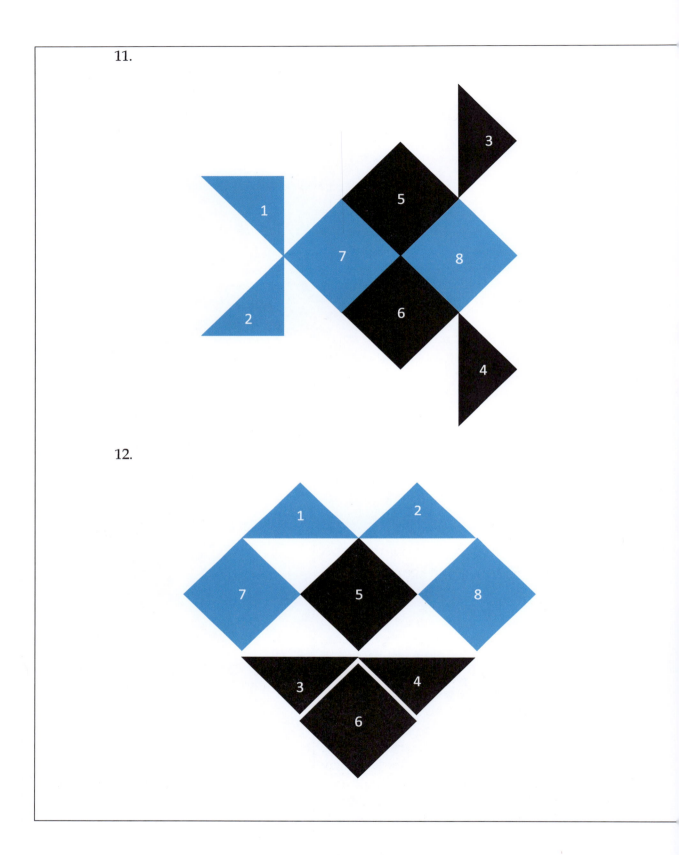

12.

13.

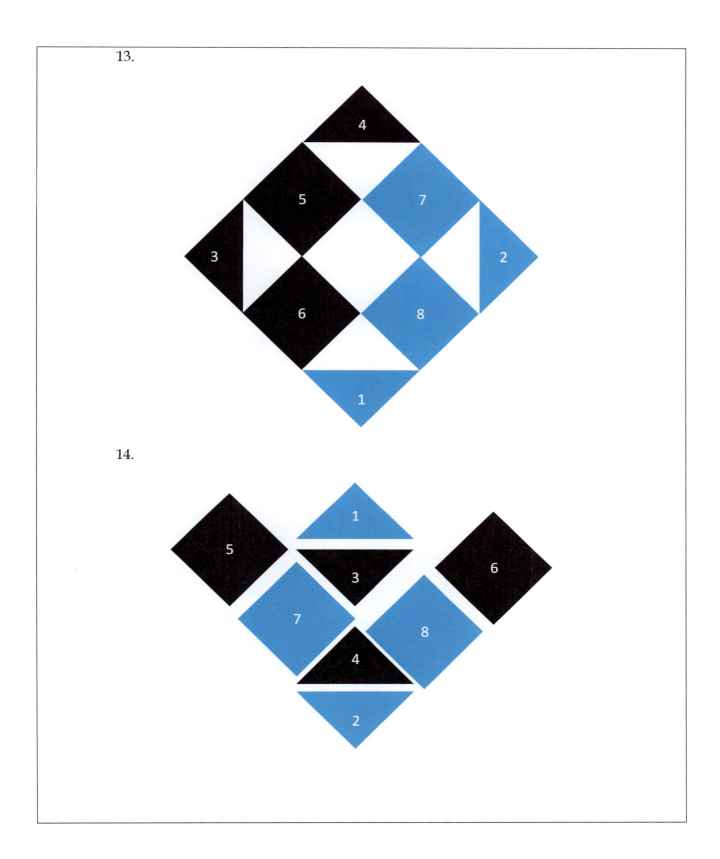

14.

15.

Section 8: Matrices

1. A. We are looking for a 4th Circle to complete the matrix.
2. C. We are looking for the 4th star with the right shade and right number of corners to complete the matrix.
3. A. We are looking for an down arrow of the same size to complete the matrix
4. A. We are looking for a slight big triangle pointed up to complete the matrix.
5. D. We are looking for an arrow to complete the 4th direction (Left, Right, Bottom and Top) to complete the matrix.
6. A. We are looking for a 3x3 squares to complete the matrix.
7. A. We are looking for a rectangle (similar to a compressed square) to complete the matrix.
8. D. We are looking for vertical arrow with a dark shade to complete the matrix.
9. B. We are looking for a light shaded triangle to complete the matrix.
10. A. We are looking for a 3 dimensional pyramid to complete the matrix.
11. D. We are looking for shaded star with pattern to complete the matrix.
12. C. We are looking for an arrow in the direction of north-east to southwest to complete the matrix.
13. C. We are looking for a shaded hexagon to complete the matrix.
14. B. We are looking for 4 stars that are shaded with patterns to complete the matrix.
15. D. We are looking for heptagon (polygon with 7 sides) to complete the pattern.
16. B. We are looking for an arrow pointing left to complete the pattern.
17. A. We are looking for a square inside a circle (positions of items are swapped from left to right.) to complete the pattern.
18. B. We are looking for 2 dark dots arranged horizontally to complete the matrix.
19. C. We are looking for a circle with right size and divided into 4 parts to complete the matrix.
20. C. We are looking for a triangle pointing down to complete the matrix.
21. B. We are looking for a square with a line and 3 prongs to complete the matrix.
22. D. We are looking for 4 circular arrows going in clockwise direction to complete the matrix.

Printed in Poland
by Amazon Fulfillment
Poland Sp. z o.o., Wrocław

31189763R00049